Published by Spy Games, LLC
646 S. Main Street #275
Cedar City, UT 84720

Copyright © Jason R. Hanson, Spy Games, LLC, 2017
All rights reserved.

Without limiting the rights under copyright reserved above, no part of this publication may be reproduced, stored in, or introduced into a retrieval system, or transmitted in any form, or by any means, without the prior written permission of both the copyright owner and the publisher of this book.

Important Publishers Note

This publication is designed to provide accurate and authoritative information in regard to the subject matter covered. If legal advice or any type of assistance is needed, please seek the services of a competent professional.

Self-defense training is potentially dangerous and should be done responsibly by all individuals. This book, produced by the Spy Games, LLC, is for informational purposes only. All technical information, instruction, and advice, reflect the beliefs of Spy Games, LLC and are intended as informational only. This book is not intended to serve as a replacement for professional instruction. By reading this book you assume all risks if you choose to use the techniques mentioned in this book. You agree to indemnify, and hold harmless the Spy Games, LLC, Jason Hanson and Danny Lane from any and all such claims and damages as a result of reading this book, which is for informational purposes only.

Introduction

Welcome to Spy Combatives.

My name is Jason Hanson. I'm a former CIA Officer and the *New York Times* bestselling author of *Spy Secrets That Can Save Your Life*. My expertise includes escape and evasion, evasive driving, and firearms, to name a few. I run a company called Spy Escape & Evasion that's been blessed to be featured on Shark Tank, the NBC Today Show, Dateline, Fox & Friends, and Rachael Ray. I created Spy Combatives to teach real people, real techniques, in real-life situations.

Working with me in Spy Combatives is Danny Lane, a highly-decorated combat Marine, retired law enforcement officer, martial arts master, and security expert with 49 years of experience.

Danny is a Master Instructor in the Chuck Norris System and has personally trained with Chuck Norris for 37 years. He has faced and survived real combat situations hundreds of times in the jungles of Vietnam as a Marine, and on the streets of America as a cop and bodyguard. He was awarded two Purple Hearts in Vietnam and the Major's Bravery Award as a police officer for saving two lives in a burning vehicle accident.

As two people who are blessed to have training from some of the best agencies in the world, Danny and I have the skills and training to provide you with self-defense skills and secrets you won't find anywhere else.

As you journey through this book, you'll learn techniques that are fast to learn, easy to comprehend, and effective in real life or death situations. The information within these pages will help you neutralize and incapacitate an attack in just seconds to keep you and your family safer.

We're Looking For a Special Group of Americans

Since Danny and I can't be in 1,000 places at once, we're currently looking for individuals who want to join the growing list of elite instructors who are teaching Spy Combatives around the world.

Certified Instructors are given marketing and business support to become successful instructors. So, not only will you help save lives, but you'll have the ability to generate extra income doing what you love.

Please note, everyone who joins our team will have to pass a background check because of the depth of training we give you.

If you're interested in more details about becoming a Spy Combatives instructor and to see if you qualify, please call 801-512-2545 or send an email to **jasonh@spyescape.com**. Thank you.

-Jason Hanson
CEO, Spy Combatives

Spy Combatives Overview

Spy Combatives was developed to combine the best of Spy, Military, and Police training to develop evolutionary, reality-based, self-defense training for men, women, and children.

Things like...

- What to do if you're duct taped to a chair during a home invasion and a criminal puts a gun to your head.

- How to conceal escape & evasion gear and the exact list of gear to carry with you.

- The crucial move you must make when someone has a gun to your back that will keep you from getting kidnapped... Or killed. (The attacker will end up with a broken arm and you'll walk away with your life.)

- How to stop an attacker and bring him to his knees if he ever puts a knife to your throat. (Not only will the attacker end up on the ground but you'll end up with his knife.)

- How a 12-cent item will allow you to pick handcuffs in less than 5 seconds giving you the chance to escape illegal restraints.

- How to defend yourself against an attacker who is throwing brutal punches. (Obviously, nobody wants to be punched in the face, but most people aren't aware of the elbow move that incapacitates an attacker and never allows them to harm you.)

- What you never, ever want to do during an active shooter situation and the exact steps to take to stop a madman with a gun.

- Hostage survival secrets usually reserved for the FBI, Special Forces and CIA.

- The "line technique" of defeating multiple home intruders. (The fact is, criminals often work together, which is why this technique is so crucial.)

And much, much more, including…

- How to become a human lie detector.

- How to escape zip ties, duct tape, rope, even handcuffs in 30 seconds or less… Without having to use a knife or sharp object.

- How to disappear without a trace.

- How to create an Escape and Evasion Kit and the critical items to include in it.

- How to use social engineering to get almost anything you want. (These are the secrets used by top intelligence agencies around the world.)

- The #1 way to create an improvised weapon if you don't have any other way to protect yourself during an emergency situation.

- How to detect and avoid surveillance like a spy

Keep in mind, Spy Combatives is not a traditional or sport-based martial art.

There are no competitions, rules or regulations. Instead, Spy Combatives is designed for the primary goal of survival in a no rules environment.

In other words, when you're in the CIA or Special Forces, the words you live by are "Alone and Unafraid."

You have to be self-reliant and know that if the "stuff hits the fan" you'll likely be on your own so you need the world's best skills to protect yourself.

That's why Spy Combatives includes reality-based scenarios that will push you to your limit and ensure if the day comes where you have to defend yourself, there's no question you'll come away with the ultimate prize – your life and the lives of the ones you love.

So, now that you understand the purpose of Spy Combatives here are some of the techniques and methods to help keep you and your family safer.

WARRIOR STANCE

The very first thing we're going to teach you is called the "Warrior Stance." While walking around during our day-to-day activity, most people walk comfortably with their feet shoulder-distance apart. Their shoulders are squared with their hips and everything is centered and natural. This makes dropping into the Warrior Stance fast and easy.

To drop to a Warrior Stance, all you have to do is bend your knees and put your hands up, palms open. Fingers are at eye level. Your feet are at a 45-degree angle to the right, and your shoulders are at a 45-degree angle to the left. What we want to do with this stance is to invite any oncoming attack towards the center of our body. We invite the attack to come down the center so we have both arms ready to defend ourselves. Your fingertips should be eye level. With your hands open, you are more relaxed. This position also offers you more coverage. Your forearms and elbows help protect your rib cage.

Practice this stance while standing and walking. Imagine a sudden attack coming at you. Quickly bend your knees and place your hands wide to block the attack. Prepare for spontaneous attacks from all angles and train your body to naturally react this way

5 DISTANCES OF COMBAT ENGAGEMENT

1. CONTACT – Grappling range, body to body, sweeps, throws, head butt, back of neck.
2. CLOSE – Open hand strikes, elbows, knees, hooks, cross, uppercuts.
3. INTERMEDIATE – Long range punches, short range kicks, front snap, cut kick.
4. LONG – Kicks, side, front thrust, stepping into other ranges.
5. OUTSIDE – Flee or close for attack with your footwork.

1. Contact Range — You are in physical contact with your attacker body to body.

2. Close Range — Close enough to attack with short range weapons.

3. Intermediate — Use long range punches and short range kicks.

4. Long Range — Use long range techniques, such as a front kick.

5. Outside Range — Requires a step forward to close the gap, or a turn for retreat.

8 ANGLES OF ATTACK AND DEFENSE

In Spy Combatives, we defend against eight different angles. We also attack at eight different angles.

Most of the time, an attack will happen fast and without warning. A combat engagement can cover many angles and distances in just seconds.

Knowing these angles and distances, and learning to instantly identify them, is crucial for your defense.

What we will do here is set the stage for you to train to encounter a real attacker. Imagine your attacker is straight ahead of you. You are standing at a distance, but centered in the middle of his body. You can now choose between 8 different angles to engage or evade the attack.

1. Straight Forward Front — Smother the attack, close the gap, and strike first.

2. 45-Degree to Right Front — Moving to the side slightly to avoid attack, and punch or hit your opponent with close-range weapons.

3. 90-Degrees to Right Side — Stepping 90-degrees to the right leaves you farther away from your opponent's attack. You'll need to counter-attack with your intermediate weapons.

4. 45-Degrees to Right Rear — Forces your opponent to move their feet to get to you, and gives you more time to plan your defense. You'll need to use long-range weapons from this angle and distance.

5. Lunging straight back 90 Degrees — Creates distance between you and the attacker, and leaves you the option to retreat or engage the attacker if they approach toward you.

6, 7, & 8 — Practice the same angles as above, starting with your left foot forward, and working the 45-degree left, 90-degree left, 45-degree rear, and straight back 90-degrees.

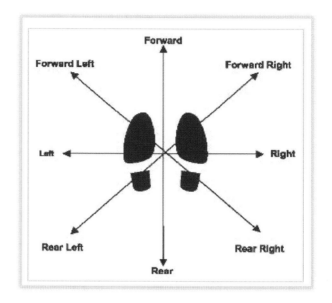

FOOTWORK: THE KEY TO FIGHTING

FOOTWORK IS THE KEY TO FIGHTING AND THE KEY TO WINNING!

You need to be able to close or retreat instantly, always controlling the range and protecting yourself. We teach footwork separately, so you can focus completely on what your feet are doing. In this section, you are going to use your footwork to close or alleviate distance between you and your opponent.

The first footwork is called a SLIDE-STEP. Start in the Warrior Stance, slide your back foot forward, and step out with your front foot. This will bring you one step closer to your opponent. Bringing your back foot forward, you can use your front foot to kick or you can step forward and punch.

During a fight, you don't want too much distance between your feet. Too much space between your feet will affect your balance, giving your opponent the opportunity to attack you. Alternate your feet, and practice moving forward and backward. Slide back to create space between you and your opponent; slide forward to close distance.

The next footwork is the reverse of what we just did and is the STEP-SLIDE. Instead of sliding the back foot first, take a step forward with the front foot, then slide the back foot forward. From here, you can kick, or push off to lunge and strike. Make sure to practice with your right and left stance forward.

The third footwork is the STEP-THROUGH. This is where the rear leg surpasses the front leg and comes forward. With this step, you can kick with the rear leg, or explode forward with your full body weight to strike or grapple.

The next footwork is the LUNGE. Pick up your front foot and push off from the rear foot at the same time. With a proper lunge, you can cover distance quickly and deliver a surprise attack. Once you disorient your opponent with a lunge, you can follow up with a kick or punch. We'll cover more attack moves in later chapters. For now, use the lunge to cover more distance, and practice lunging forward and back until you know how much distance you can cover or create.

Practice lunging backward by picking up your rear leg and exploding backward to evade an attack.

After you master each footwork, practice combinations with them to cover even more distance. Use each of the movements together, forwards and backwards, to train your mind and body on proper footwork technique. Take the time to learn the footwork and make it second nature to you. In a fight, you must be focused on your attacker, not on what your feet are doing.

VITAL AND VULNERABLE TARGETS OF THE BODY

Knowing where to attack on the human body can quickly neutralize an attacker. It takes skill to master the angle and direction of each strike, as well as knowing what strike to use on each vital and vulnerable target. This skill will come through practice, experience, and a knowledge of each of the weapons. My favorite places to strike are the eyes, ears, throat, and neck.

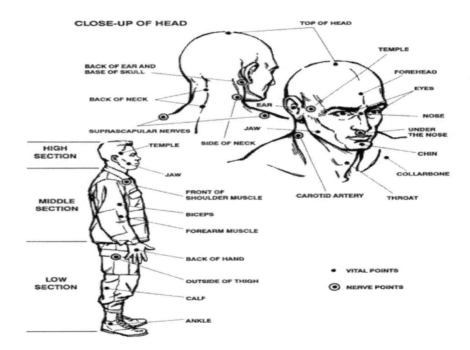

ZONE BLOCKING

Most people naturally react to a punch by throwing their hands up to block, which is exactly what we want you to do. We want you to follow your natural instincts, using your hands and arms to cover specific areas of the body we will call ZONES.

To Zone Block, keep both hands wide and directly towards the attack. Sometimes you will cross your arms to reinforce your blocks and sometimes you will have one up and one down in what we call a general block.

Let's say someone is attacking you with a swift punch to the left side of your face. You would lift both hands up wide to meet the attack. Practice blocking with a partner. There are **nine zones** we want you to learn to defend:

1. Left High

2. Left Middle

3. Left Low

4. Underneath

5. Right High

6. Right Middle

7. Right Low

8. Overhead

9. Straight Stab or Strike to Mid-Section

SOFT BLOCKS AND HARD BLOCKS DEFINED

Let's say your attacker is a strong male. If he throws a hard punch at your face, some people will teach you to try and counter with a hard block. That method is only effective if you are stronger than your opponent.

The Spy Combatives philosophy is to use a soft block to redirect the attack. If your attacker punches with his right arm, you should step right and use soft hands to move the punch away from you. It can be as simple as moving his arm a few inches off course to make him miss.

Use HARD BLOCKS against a grab or a push. You need to be aggressive to knock their hands off of you. You become the aggressor at that that point.

HOW TO ESCAPE DUCT TAPE

Every single day, people are tied up and bound during kidnappings and home invasions. If you don't know how to escape these situations, horrible things can happen to you. We will teach you how to escape duct tape, zip ties, and rope.

We are going to start with duct tape first because duct tape is a criminal's favorite way to kidnap and restrain people all over the world. The reason criminals love duct tape is because it's easy to access. You can go to almost any hardware store and get duct tape. Unfortunately, most people have no idea how to escape duct tape. Often times, people mentally give up when they find themselves bound, and we don't want this to happen to you.

We're going to start with your hands, and what to do if your wrists are duct taped.

These escape methods are very easy to do, and we have successfully trained people from ages 4 to 85. Anyone can do this, male or female, and it has nothing to do with strength.

The key to escaping duct tape is to keep your elbows as close together as possible (while being taped). This is easy to do when a criminal has you. They're not going to notice you trying to keep your elbows together because you look submissive when you're doing this. Additionally, criminals want to kidnap you quickly. They want to bind your hands so they can throw you inside of a van or drag you off in a car. They're not going to sit there for 10 minutes while they duct tape you.

When most people find their wrists bound in duct tape, they try and pull it apart. No matter how strong they are, most people will never be able to pull their hands apart when taped, and that's why they mentally give up. To quickly escape in less than two seconds, however, all you have to do is raise your hands as high above your head as possible, then pull down quickly while separating your hands and throwing your elbows behind you.

In Spy Combatives, we have our students practice this several times. Again, you place your taped hands up as high as possible. As you start bringing them down, pull your hands apart, and throw your elbows behind you like you are slapping your hips.

While teaching this escape, we have seen one common mistake that is important to note before you practice at home. Some people will bring their hands down and THEN try to pull their hands apart. And they can't escape.

Remember that as soon as you start bringing your hands down, you also have to start pulling your hands apart. Again, it has nothing to do with strength. It's about creating the precise angle needed to tear the tape. When you pull down as described above, you create the angle that tears the tape.

Some criminals will duct tape you around the wrists, but then also go the opposite way between your hands. This only makes it *appear* harder to escape. (The Israeli Special Forces love to use this method.)

If you ever find yourself in this position, the good news is you can use the exact same escape as before. The duct tape may feel tighter, but nothing changes in the technique.

It may feel like you can't move at all, but you'll still put your hands high above your head and come down in the exact same way as before.

This action will still bust the loop around your wrists. The middle loop will stay there, but it won't matter because your hands will be free. Once the first loop is gone, the second loop is just a circle of tape between your freed hands.

After you escape, you can employ the tactics we're teaching you here in Spy Combatives to defend yourself. (All Spy Combatives instructors get training videos showing this escape and all of the techniques in this book.)

ESCAPE DUCT TAPE USING A WALL OR EDGE SURFACE

If your arms are injured, or for some other reason, you can't get the correct angle for the first escape, this second technique will come into play. Let's assume that your wrists are taped up and you can't get the correct angle to break free. For this second technique to work you need to find some type of 90-degree angle. It could be a window seal, a table edge, the corner of a wall, or anything else with a good edge.

For this example, we'll use the corner of a wall. Place your hands completely flat with the wall, keeping your forearms parallel to the wall (your wrists *and* elbows need to be close to the wall). Once your hands are flat, press against the wall while using a sawing motion up and down along the corner. This will allow you to escape in under five seconds, making this a great alternative if you're unable to use the first method.

ESCAPE BEING DUCT TAPED TO A CHAIR

Too often during home invasions, criminals will duct tape people to chairs. They like this method because you are stuck in a chair while they go through and ransack or destroy your house. Sometimes they leave after they get what they came for, but other times they come back and harm the person, kill them, or do horrible things to them.

There are stories all the time on the news of people being duct taped in this way, and we are going to teach you how to escape.

To practice this at home, have someone duct tape you like a criminal would: Simply duct tape right around your chest to secure you to the chair. Most people in this position try and scoot forward, or they kind of scurry or shuffle forward in the chair; but it really doesn't do much. The following escape will show you what you can do to escape in mere seconds, just like other duct tape escape method.

You don't want to go forward and shimmy or move. The best way to escape is by creating an angle that tears it, just like you did with your hands. To accomplish this, jolt forward quickly, as if to put your head between your legs. Imagine you're on an airplane, and all of a sudden, you feel like you're going to throw up. If you feel sick on a plane, you put your head between your legs and you're puking in the barf bag.

That is the same position you will assume to escape being duct taped to a chair. But you're going to jolt and do it quickly. Take a little lean back and then quickly lean forward, putting your head between your knees. Practice the movement first without duct tape, and then with the tape. You now know how to escape in seconds if you are ever duct taped to a chair.

ESCAPE HANDS, CHEST, AND ANKLES TIED WITH DUCT TAPE

For another duct tape escape, we will teach you how to escape if you are taped to a chair *and* your hands and feet are bound. This type of restraint is really only used by criminals that are willing to spend a *lot* of time, and *really* want to make sure you aren't going anywhere.

Perhaps, if you are a well-known celebrity or political figure, and you are a potential target (not just some random home invasion), you may find yourself needing this escape method someday.

In this position, your chest, hands, and feet are all duct taped. It will feel very tight. Many people (who don't know what you now know) will mentally give up in this case, but you will be able to get free in no time at all. And, when you do, your goal is to get out of the house, get to safety, and call 9-1-1, since, in many cases, the criminal has left you alone while they are in your master bedroom going through your drawers and other belongings.

The first thing you'll do is quickly jolt forward to free your chest using the escape you just learned. After your chest is free, you can concentrate on freeing your hands.

Stand up, raising your hands as high as you can, then bring your hands down quickly and pull them apart as if you are trying to slap your hips.

Remember, if you are unable to free your hands this way, you know how to use a corner surface to escape.

Last is the feet. The feet are very easy to escape if they have duct tape around them. All you're going to do is squat down and point your toes outwards. In other words, your toes should not be pointing straight ahead, they should form a V-shape as you quickly squat to the ground.

And, if that doesn't work, your hands are free now and you can just bend down and tear the tape. But, the quickest way to escape tape around your feet is to squat while pointing your toes outwards. This technique will quickly "pop" the tape.

As you can see, even if you were duct taped almost everywhere, you can escape in under 5 seconds.

ESCAPE HANDS TIED WITH ZIP TIES

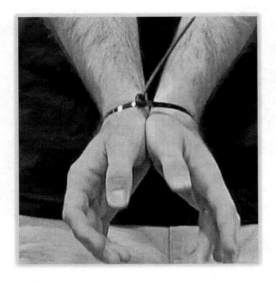

Now we'll go over two ways to escape from zip ties. The first way requires you to get the angle perfectly (if you do not get the angle right, it can be uncomfortable). The secret is to position the lock in the center of your hands and make sure the zip tie is tight. (See the picture on the left.)

Obviously, if the lock is not in the center, you will need to move it there. You can grab the zip tie with your teeth and pull the lock until it is on the top between your hands.

For practicing, we recommend you have someone help you put the lock in the center because it can hurt your teeth to pull on the zip tie. But, in an emergency, you won't mind putting some pressure on your teeth if it's going to save your life.

Once the zip tie is tight and centered, use the same movements to escape the zip ties that you would use for escaping duct tape. Put your hands high above your head and pull down while throwing your elbows behind you or slapping your own hips.

The only difference is that you have to do this one with more strength because, obviously, zip ties are stronger than duct tape.

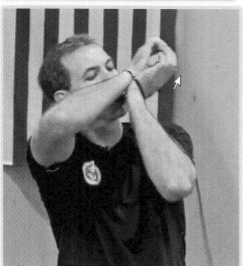

The good news is, even if you can't do it in training, it doesn't necessarily mean you won't be able to do it when you need to. In a life or death situation, you'll have an adrenaline surge, amping you up and making you stronger… Just like the stories you've heard about grandma lifting a car off of a child. In a crisis, adrenaline is on your side.

The second way to escape zip ties is by using paracord (AKA parachute cord.) For this escape, it's not necessary for the zip tie to be as tight or the lock to be in the center of your hands. Let's say that you've tried the first zip tie escape method but you can't get out. That's when you use paracord. Paracord can cut through all kinds of things (including zip ties and rope).

Thread your paracord through the zip tie and attach one loop to your left foot and another loop to your right foot. It is important to remember to keep the paracord at the very bottom of the zip tie, so it's not touching your skin. Otherwise, the friction from the paracord will burn you while trying to escape.

Once the paracord is looped onto your feet, you're going pull your hands up to keep the paracord tight, then use bicycling motions with your feet. This movement will quickly cut through the zip ties, allowing you to flee, use moves to defend yourself, disarm your attacker, or do whatever else needs to be done.

Next, we'll teach you how to escape rope.

HANDS TIED WITH ROPE

Another popular restraint method criminals love to use (in addition to duct tape and zip ties) is rope. Later in the Spy Combatives series, we'll practice drills with somebody is coming at you with a knife or a gun, and you'll have to escape rope and then disarm them to protect yourself.

Remember the first duct tape escape you learned and how it was important to keep your elbows as close together as possible?

Rope is the complete opposite. You want to keep your elbows to your side (spread apart, touching your rib cage, rather than close together) and bring your hands close to your body. Criminals will tie the rope around your wrists, but with this escape, it doesn't matter how hard they tie you up if your elbows are spread apart when they're doing it. This is because it creates false space in the wrists. If your elbows and hands are together (like with the duct tape method), you won't have that same curve of the wrists to create false space. But if your elbows are at your side, when the time comes to escape, you just straighten out your hands, putting them flat (with your palms touching), and shimmy, shimmy, shimmy to free your hands. Flat hands will have enough space to slide out of the rope. Even if a criminal is using paracord or a much thinner rope, you can still create that space around your wrists that will allow you to escape. Now, with paracord or similar materials, you may get some rope burn, but in a life and death situation, the burn is well worth it.

ESCAPE HANDCUFFS WITH A BOBBY PIN

We're now going to show you multiple ways to escape handcuffs using a bobby pin and a hair barrette. You'll need to make these items ahead of time, so take a moment before going over the exercises to pre-make your tools.

First, we'll start with a bobby pin. You need to make it one long piece of metal. So in other words, just take the bend out so you'll have a straight piece of metal here. Next, you'll notice there is a bumpy end and a smooth end (we want to work with the smooth end only) and there is a nub on each end.

Take the nub off of the smooth end by clamping down with a pair of pliers and pulling (it comes right off).

Next, you need to put a small 45-degree bend on the smooth end. It's a very tiny bend, maybe 1/8 of an inch, at 45-degrees. So you're not doing much at all. If you have a 90-degree bend, that is way too much.

For training purposes, do not put the handcuffs on the first time you are practicing this. If you are right handed, you'll have your bobby pin in your right hand and your handcuffs in your left. Notice the key hole and also the little notch to the side of it that juts off of the right. The only area we're working in is that little notch that juts off to the right. You don't want to have anything near the key hole.

Take your bobby pin, with the scoop up like a tiny shovel, and stick it right in that little notch until you hit metal. Then pull straight down and the cuffs should come open.

Sometimes handcuffs are stiff. If you pull down and it doesn't open, try pushing to your right and it will open. Because of the amount of force you're using, this will likely take the bend out of your tool. So, if you're going to a very dangerous place, you'll want to have multiple bobby pins with you.

Use pliers to recreate the angle you need after each practice.

ESCAPE HANDCUFFS WITH A HAIR BARRETTE

Now I'll show you the hair barrette method, which is easier for most people. Even if you prefer the bobby pin, you never know how the cuffs are going to be on, so it's best to have two different ways to escape.

Just like we had to prepare the bobby pin a certain way, the barrette also requires you to prepare your tool ahead of time.

Locate the metal piece in the middle of the barrette and bend it all the way up until it snaps and falls off. You should now have a hair barrette that has no metal middle piece.

Next, find the round top where it curves, the thickest part. Bend this thick part back and forth until it snaps off. You want to snap it off to leave the barrette in the shape of a V. The edges will most likely be curved. Use pliers to straighten out these pieces of metal—that way they're not curved like they were—and once you're happy with how straight they are, you will have turned the barrette into a shim. You'll use this shim to block the teeth on the handcuffs, allowing them to open easily.

Once again, practice first with the cuffs off. Hold the cuffs in your non-dominant hand and practice using the shim with your dominant hand. Making sure the teeth are facing upwards, use one hand and only one end of the hair barrette—whichever end you want.

For the escape, shove the hair barrette right where the teeth go in. This action alone, however, does nothing. You'll first need to push down on the teeth and then immediately follow shoving the hair barrette all the way in. When you push down on the teeth, it creates the momentum that allows you to shove the hair barrette down. First push. Then shove the barrette in. It stops at the circle joint—as you'll see—hold it in place and lift the cuff off of your hand. This is possible because the shim is blocking the teeth.

So, again, that is why you should always carry a hair barrette *and* a bobby pin because you never know which direction, or from what angle the cuffs will be placed.

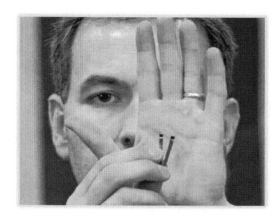

The picture above shows how the hair barrette should end up looking.

ESCAPE ROPE WITH PARACORD

You already know the fastest way to escape rope by creating false space so you can quickly slide your hands out. But, here's Plan B if you can't get that method to work. Put simply, use the paracord the same way I taught you to escape zip ties:

Loop it through the bottom of the rope to avoid rope burn, sit down and put the paracord loops on your feet, and bicycle quickly until the rope breaks.

DEFENSE AGAINST SIDE HEADLOCK

The Side Headlock is one of the most often used techniques by street fighters. They want to trap your head and beat your face in. Below is one of the defenses for the side headlock. FIRST, you have to stop the arm that is hitting your face by blocking it. SECOND, go around behind their back with your left arm and trap their arm. THIRD, you strike their groin to slow stun them. This will give you a chance to loosen their grip on your neck. FOURTH, bring your arm over their shoulder and claw their face. FIFTH, once they are off balance, drive a downward elbow to their face or chest.

CLOSE QUARTER COMBAT
FRONT CHOKE GUILLOTINE

Use the Front Choke Guillotine when someone is in close or contact range. It also works great when the attacker tries to come in for a take down. The object is to get around the neck from the front, and wrap their neck into a trachea choke. There are many variations of this choke, both standing and on the ground. In the pictures below, I strike with a cross elbow to the jaw, and then do another reverse strike to the other side of his neck with my forearm. This stuns him just before I wrap the neck. Then, I go around the neck, and lock it tight under the wind pipe. I lock my right hand onto my left arm to create a strong vice.

CLOSE QUARTER COMBAT
CHOKES: REAR NAKED & STANDING ARM BAR

Chokes are taught in the military more than in law enforcement because of the possibility of causing death and civil liability. In real life situations, you can use these self-defense tactics, but make sure the force is reasonable and justified. In the Rear Naked Choke, I am cutting off the oxygen to the brain and the blood supply at the same time. This will incapacitate an attacker in a few seconds. You can adjust the amount of force you apply depending on their resistance. I have him locked in with my arms, using my head to create even more leverage on his neck. I press forward on his neck to render him unconscious in seconds.

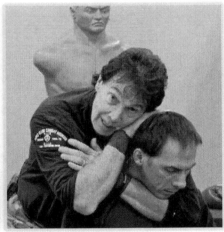

Below is a tactic I used in law enforcement. It is called the Spin Around Arm Bar. Push and pull on their shoulders to spin them around. This is done fast and hard. Create a bar across their neck with your arm, and bring the other hand up to create pressure on the carotid or the wind pipe to get them to comply. The carotid choke is legal in law enforcement.

CLOSE QUARTER COMBAT
STANDING TRIANGLE CHOKE

The Standing Triangle Choke is a great tactic to get an attacker under control fast! Here, I smack his right arm up and slip under. At the same time, I strike the other side of his neck with a firm hand. Then, I grasp my hands together and trap his arm against his neck. I create pressure on his neck and activate a nerve at the base of his skull with my radial bone. This will weaken his legs and you can take him to the ground quickly.

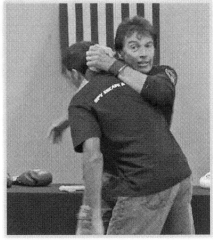

CLOSE QUARTER COMBAT
DEFENSE AGAINST THE SHOOT TAKE DOWN

In the street, most fights end up on the ground. This technique will educate you on how to defend yourself against being taken down in the first place. When the attacker strikes, I smack his head hard with a palm heel. This will break his focus and his direction. Then, I go around his neck with my other hand and create the choke. I lock it in tight as you can see and stretch him out until he submits.

CLOSE QUARTER COMBAT
DEFENSE AGAINST STREET PUNCHER

Defending against a fast, powerful street fighter is frightening. Any single punch landed in the right place can knock you out, and it's impossible to block every punch. The only solution is to create distance to get away, or close distance to get close to the attacker and smother his punches. I use the terms COVER, SMOTHER, and SLIP TO SIDE. Here, I get close (right into his chest) so he can't hit me hard. Then I slip around to a side control. I break his balance by pulling in at his hip bones. I let him fight and wear himself down trying to get loose. After he slows down I can then execute the take down, mount to submit him or pound him if necessary.

CONCEALING GEAR FOR TRAVEL

Depending on where you travel, especially if you go overseas to the more dangerous areas of the world, you need to know how to conceal escape and evasion gear. That gear can include money, a razor blade, lock pick sets, bobby pins, hair barrettes, handcuff keys – pretty much anything you want to conceal. One of the ways I conceal gear is my Escape & Evasion Gun Belt. **(www.CovertBelt.com.)**

The Escape & Evasion Gun Belt has three different pockets where I can store gear. I've traveled all over the world with the belt. In the first pocket, I have a universal handcuff key and a lock pick set, including a tension wrench and an L-rake, so I can pick locks. In the middle pocket, I have a bobby pin and hair barrette. When I'm not flying (and not going through airport security), I have a razor blade in the belt, too. I also carry several $20 bills in the belt for emergency cash.

In addition to using a gun belt, another way to conceal gear is athletic tape. If you've played sports, you've probably injured your finger, jammed, or broken a finger. What you can do with this athletic tape is that you can tape two of your fingers together. You can take a handcuff key, you can take a razor blade, you can take pretty much anything you want, and you can just roll the tape around it multiple times.

Who's going to question somebody walking around with two fingers taped together? No one. It's a common sight that we are used to seeing when someone has an injury. Not only can you tape your fingers with a handcuff key, you can also use the large bandages that you stick on your arm and hide all types of weapons underneath.

If you really want to take it to another level, apply some red food dye. If someone sees a bloody bandage, they're not going to want to tear it off and say, "Hey, do you have a handcuff key? Do you have a razor blade?" So, use bandages of all types to conceal gear.

Another option is to use the tags in your clothing. You have a tag on your shirt. You have a tag on the inside of your pants. You can take a little piece of duct tape and you can tape a razor blade or a handcuff key on the inside of that tag.

Besides tags, you can also use a safety pin. Attach the pin to some type of baggie (large or small), drop the bag right in your pants, then put the safety pin through your clothes, in the front and the back. You can put all sorts of things in the bag.

If you don't want to use a bag, then you can just take the safety pin, put it through the handcuff key, and pin it right to your clothes.

Some other ideas to conceal items: You can tape items to the bottom of your feet, you can tape items to the tongue of your shoe, and you can put handcuff keys on the end of your shoelaces. You can get creative as you want with gear and ways to store it. You are only limited by your imagination.

GROUND & POUND WITH TRAINING DUMMY

Training with a bag or dummy is important for developing power and technique. Here, I am running one of our students, Richard, through a series of drills from the mount.

He can strike and practice his submissions without any complaints or injuries from the training dummy.

TRAINING WITH BOB

Using a training device such as BOB (Body Opponent Bag) is great for developing focus, power, and realistic training.

BOB is a great addition to your home gym. I use BOB mostly for my open hand strikes, knees, elbows, and lower level kicks.

BLOCKING POWER KICKS

I use soft blocks against hard kicks. I can also use footwork to create distance to clear the kick, redirect it, and then counter.

If your timing is sharp, you can counter while the attacker is mid-kick.

Surviving a Knife Attack

Every self-defense situation is dangerous and stressful, but defending against someone with a knife raises the emotion to the highest level. Most experts agree that they would rather be faced with a gun instead of a knife. I feel the same way.

In Spy Combatives, we are going to use the KISS formula. We will teach you tactics that you can learn fast.

It is very difficult to disarm anyone with a knife especially someone that is in a highly-agitated state of mind and wants to kill.

In my military and police career, I had several actual life-and-death encounters with a knife. As a combat Marine, we were trained to fight with the K-Bar and bayonet in case of a hand-to-hand encounter with the enemy. I had such an encounter in Vietnam when my unit was overrun by the North Vietnamese Army in an operation near Laos.

The sappers charged through our lines in the jungle and it was every Marine for himself. I found myself fighting with a sapper wired with explosives, hand-to-hand in my fox hole with only my knife. Sadly, I had to take his life to save mine.

As a Police Defensive Tactics Instructor, I teach officers how to use the knife as a weapon first and then how to defend. As a cop, I had to disarm a few bad guys over the years on the street when they wanted to cut me. With my training, I didn't feel deadly force was necessary at that time and it all turned out well.

OFFENSIVE KNIFE FIGHTING- 9 CUTS

Below are the 9 different angles I teach to use in a combat situation. Each cut can be used individually or in combination with others. I use horizontal, vertical and diagonal cuts. Within 9 cuts, there are 3 different

levels: head, body, and legs.

ZONE BLOCKING

A knife attack happens fast. Sometimes it is dark and you can't see. You may be lucky enough to see a flash of the weapon before you are cut. I teach you to block in zones so you have a chance to block any attack in that general area. You must learn to block all 8 zones, as well as your center. Practice with your partner coming at you slowly at first, and then rapidly over time. Once you learn to block the zones you can then concentrate more on seizing the weapon arm. This allows you to control the weapon.

The object is to seize the arm holding the weapon. Once you seize the arm, follow our formula for disarming.

Seize, Control, Close, Attack, Takedown, and Disarm. Be sure to seize the arm with both hands facing opposite of each other to secure their arm.

DEFENSE AGAINST A SLASH

A slash is a circular attack, usually to the neck or upper body. We teach to bend inside the angle of the cut and engage with a zone block. One you seize the arm, slide up and lock the arm out. Then you can go to work attacking with knees, head butts, and taking them to the ground and disarming the weapon.

Zone Blocking   Seize Arm   Close & Lock it in

Shot to Neck   Knees to Stun   Stomp foot take down

DEFENSE AGAINST A STAB

 This is a must-learn tactic. Practice having your training partner stab quickly at you. Avoid the stab by sliding back quickly and sucking in your diaphragm. At the same time, smack the knife down to disarm or seize it. Once you have seized control of the knife, close, attack, and disarm as previously taught.

DEFENSE AGAINST KNIFE TO NECK FROM BEHIND

In this situation, timing is everything. You have to wait for the right moment to make your move. Step away from the knife, turn your neck, and use your neck muscle to create space. At the same time, get your hand on their wrist to keep the knife from your throat. When you're proficient with these techniques, the elbow should also be delivered at the same time to stun the attacker. Back fist his nose and strike the groin. This gives you time to step back and snap his elbow over your shoulder.

After that, I drop his arm off my shoulder and turn left to drop him to the ground. If the knife is still in his hand, I spread his arm out and put my knee on his elbow to disarm the knife.

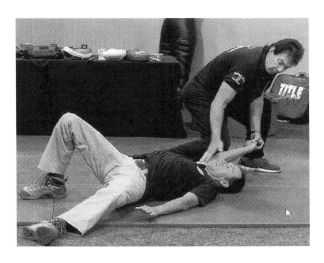

DEFENSE AGAINST KNIFE TO BACK OPTION #1

Spin, step back and across with your left foot, and parry the knife away from your back. Continue your parry until you create a vice with your arm pinning his arm and the knife. The movements have to be quick and fluid. Strike the attacker in the head and then come back to disarm the knife.

DEFENSE AGAINST KNIFE TO BACK #2

Spin, step back and across with your left foot, and strike the attacker's neck with a ridge hand to the neck to stun him. Go around the neck as you spin into the hip throw position. Drive your hips backwards, and throw the attacker to the ground. Create a vice with your legs and rip the weapon out.

DEFENSE AGAINST KNIFE TO THROAT

This could be very useful in a mugging situation. The thing to remember here, is to cooperate and give them what they want to avoid the risk of dying. If the opportunity arises, however, and your decision is to act, here is something you can do. If they tell you to put your hands up, do so, but slowly. Here, I have mine up just above his arms. You notice my right hand is in between his arms. This gives me the angle to attack when I am ready.

I made my decision to react by turning my body to the left, and at the same time, grabbing the weapon hand and striking his arm. This clears the weapon from my neck. I immediately strike him with a hammer fist to the neck to stun him, and then come back to his arm with a reverse chop to the radial nerve. If the weapon doesn't drop, you have many other options for disarming. This whole sequence should be done in about a second.

DEFENSE AGAINST KNIFE TO THROAT REVERSE GRIP

Here, I grab his arm with the weapon, push it back, and pin it into his chest. Then, I move in close and attack with a head butt, step on his foot, and get him to the ground.

DEFENSE AGAINST KNIFE TO GUT

If the attacker comes up to your gut with a knife from his belt or back, and you don't have time to slide back, just drop down and block the arm with a low forearm block. Keep your arm 90-degrees to ensure his arm doesn't slide off and come up to your neck with the knife. Immediately go into the control technique you learned previously to lock his arm and weapon in.

Here, I use a wrist lock to start the disarm. Kick or do an arm bar from here.

DEFENSE AGAINST KNIFE TO HEAD

Here, the attack is coming from overhead. I bend or lean to the left and parry the arm away from me downward. I use a circular motion to seize the arm, and continue into a step under shoulder lock. This is used in Aikido and Ju-Jitsu. Then I have him under my control, and can break his wrist or take him to the ground.

RETURN TO SENDER

The Return to Sender knife defense is very important, as it directs the knife attack back into the attacker.

I block the attack with my right arm, then come inside and strike the bend of his elbow with my left arm. At the same time, I grab and twist his arm down and around into his own body.

Final Notes

Remember, this is just a small taste of the complete Spy Combatives curriculum. If you're accepted as an instructor, you'll be fully trained including surveillance detection skills, how to be a human lie detector, hostage rescue techniques, and much, much more.

You'll also get our vast resources including marketing, technical and business expertise that have helped us to be able to already train thousands of people all over the world.

Please call 801-512-2545 for more information on becoming a Spy Combatives instructor or email **jasonh@spyescape.com**.

Thank you and stay safe.

-Jason Hanson

Made in the USA
San Bernardino, CA
21 December 2019